Copyright © 2021 Clavis Publishing Inc., New York.

Originally published as *Wilde dieren in de sneeuw. Dierenprentenboek met verhalen en informatie*
in Belgium and the Netherlands by Clavis Uitgeverij, 2018
English translation from the Dutch by Clavis Publishing Inc., New York

Visit us on the Web at www.clavis-publishing.com.

Wild Animals in the Snow. A Picture Book about Animals with Stories and Information
compiled by Marja Baeten and the World Wildlife Fund, and illustrated by Gertie Jaquet

ISBN 978-1-60537-720-9

This book was printed in April 2021 at Nikara, M. R. Štefánika 858/25, 963 01 Krupina, Slovakia.

First Edition
10 9 8 7 6 5 4 3 2 1

WILD ANIMALS
in the
Snow

A Picture Book about Animals with Stories and Information

Compiled by
**Marja Baeten
and WWF**

Illustrated by
Gertie Jaquet

Clavis

NEW YORK

Index

Matt, the Flying Penguin

Lucas Arnoldussen

Matt thinks it's cold today. Very, very, very cold.

The little penguin snuggles closer to his mommy.

Mmm, that's nice and warm. And he's sheltered from the icy wind.

"When I grow up, I'll just fly away from here," says Matt.

"I'll fly to a nice, warm place. I'm a bird for a reason, right?"

"You're a bird indeed. But you can't fly, just like me, Daddy,
and all the other penguins," says Mommy.

"But . . . what do we need these things for?" Matt asks, as he flaps his little wings.

"You'll see later," says Mommy. "Just be patient."

Matt looks at two flying albatrosses. They fly through the air with their
huge black-and-white wings. He wishes he could do the same thing.

Mommy and Daddy don't even try to fly, he thinks.
Neither do any of the other penguins. Matt sneaks away from the group of penguins.
When no one can see him, he stands firmly on two legs. He counts. 1 . . . 2 . . . 3!
As hard as he can, Matt waves his small wings up and down, but nothing happens.
He doesn't soar through the air like an albatross. He doesn't even get off the ground.

Disappointed, Matt lets his head hang.
He thinks, *maybe penguins just aren't good at taking off.*
But maybe they're very good at floating through the air. How do I get up in the air?

Then Matt sees the big ice cliff.
It's the cliff where Mommy doesn't allow him to go.
It's much too steep and too close to
the dangerous sea and especially . . . far too high!
Matt knows what he has to do.
He walks to the cliff and starts to climb.
It's a long, slippery climb.
When Matt is finally at the top, he carefully looks
down over the edge. There's the dangerous sea . . .

Then the little penguin sees the two albatrosses flying over.
I'm a bird, Matt thinks bravely. *So, I can fly too!*
He jumps off the cliff. He flaps his wings like a real bird. He flies!
Oh dear . . . Matt starts to fall. Faster and faster . . . SPLASH!
The little penguin falls into the sea.

The water feels less cold than Matt thought.
There's no ice-cold wind underwater.
Matt starts to like the water.
When he flaps his wings, he shoots like a rocket!
This is fun, he thinks. *The sea isn't dangerous at all!*
Suddenly someone grabs his neck. *Oh no!* Matt thinks.
Matt is lifted out of the water, and placed safely on the ice.
Who did that? he thinks.
It's Mommy! She looks angry and proud at the same time.
"Penguins can't fly, can they, Mommy?" Matt asks softly.
"No," Mommy laughs. "But we can swim best with our wings. Shall we do it again, together?"

11

The Emperor Penguin

Passport

Habitat: on the ice of
the South Pole
Weight: up to 82 pounds
Height: up to 43 inches
Favorite food: fish, squid,
and shrimp
About them: penguins walk
slow, but they're very fast
underwater.

Fun fact
The emperor penguin
is the biggest of all
the penguins.

A mommy emperor penguin lays only one egg. The daddy penguin gets the egg and balances it on his feet for over two months! He keeps the egg very warm with his layer of skin.

While the male is hatching the egg, the female looks for food in the sea. After almost three months, the mommy comes back with food she brings up to feed the new chicks.

If it's very cold and the wind blows hard, the penguins huddle close to each other. This helps them stay nice and warm.

Penguins can recognize each other by their call, even if there are thousands of other penguins in one area. Each call is slightly different with every penguin.

Smokey, the Arctic Fox

Marie-José Balm

Seven small arctic foxes crawl out of the hole one by one.
Seven small arctic foxes flash their eyes and see the world for the first time.
It's cold and vast and white.
Seven small arctic foxes play in the snow. They romp around.
They scream, "Catch me if you can!"
Six small arctic foxes are white.
But the smallest one is blue-gray. His name is Smokey.

Smokey runs away, farther away than the other arctic foxes.
Suddenly there's no ground under his paws. He sinks away
and drops through the soft snow. He falls and falls.
Where is he? Where are the others? Smokey sharpens his ears. He hears water drops.
Smokey is sniffing. Water, snow, and ice. He looks around. There's light in the distance.
Smokey runs towards it. This must be the world.

There's the vast, white world.
But . . . where are the others?
A big fish swims in the sea.
He jumps out of the water.
Smokey runs towards it. "Do you
know where the others are?" he calls.
"Which others? Who do you belong to?
I don't know a land animal like you."

The fish dives into the water.
I'm a land animal, Smokey thinks.
A heavy animal lies on a rock.
It has a mustache and a fishtail.
Smokey runs there. "Do you know
where the others are?" he asks.
"Which others? Who do you belong
to? I don't know an animal with
four paws like you."

The walrus falls asleep.
I have four paws, Smokey thinks.
A white animal with a black nose
and four legs walks on the hill.
Smokey runs towards it. "Do you know
where the others are?"
"Which others? Who do you belong to?
I don't know a gray animal like you."

The polar bear trudges further.
I'm gray, Smokey thinks. Then he sees
an animal that looks a bit like him.
Smokey runs towards it. "Do you
know where the others are?"
"Which others? Who do you belong to?
I don't know an arctic fox like you."

"So, I'm an arctic fox?" asks Smokey.

"You're an arctic fox, and I'm a wolf," the wolf says. "But I've never seen a blue-gray arctic fox. I'm your distant uncle. We're far relatives."

"Far relatives?" Smokey asks. It starts to snow. He shivers.

Smokey feels small and alone. "Where do I go now?" he asks.

"Back to the arctic foxes," the wolf says.

"I'll take you home because I'm your uncle."

Off they go.
The big wolf is leading the way.
The small arctic fox follows.
The snow is falling. The storm is roaring.
It's a long, far journey.
Finally, they see the den.
"You've arrived. Bye, small arctic fox," says the wolf.
"Thank you, Uncle Wolf," says Smokey.
He dives into the den. There are the others. He's home!
Seven small arctic foxes are nice and warm against their mommy.
Six are white. The smallest one is blue-gray. And that's Smokey.

The Arctic Fox

Passport

Habitat: **near the North Pole**
Weight: **up to 9 pounds**
Height: **a bit shorter than the common fox**
Length: **22 inches, tail 12 inches**
Favorite food: **lemmings (a type of hamsters), birds, mice, and arctic rabbits**
About them: **he has a black edge around the eyes.**

In winter, the arctic fox has twice as much hair as in summer. This way, it doesn't suffer from the cold.

The arctic fox digs a hole deep under the snow. It sometimes sleeps in the deep hole during the winter. It's less cold under the snow.

In winter, the arctic fox is white. You hardly see it in the snow. In summer, it gets new brown hair.

The arctic fox doesn't get cold even at 60 degrees below zero. When it sleeps, it puts its tail over its snout like a blanket.

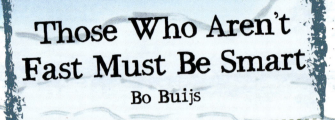

Harp the seal is proud
that he's very fast.
He laughs at anyone who
swims slower than he does.
"Haha! What a slow-poke you are!"
he says to Starfish.
"You really are a snail!" to Sea Snail.
"You're slower than a stone!" to Sea Crab.
 One day, Sea Crab has enough of it.
 She writes Harp a note:

Dear Harp,

Meet me tomorrow at the
seaweed grove by the big boulder.

Love,
Sea Crab

Harp is curious about what Sea Crab has to say.

He races straight to the seaweed grove the next morning.

Sea Crab is already waiting for him next to a sign with a starfish on it.

"What's the sign for?" asks Harp.

"We're going to have a competition, and this sign is the start,"
explains Sea Crab. "We'll see who's the fastest."

For a moment, Harp thinks he misunderstood.

"A competition to see who's the fastest? Between you and me?"

Sea Crab nods. "Exactly."

Harp bursts out laughing. "But you're the slowest of them all.
When you start running, you stumble over your own long legs!"

But Sea Crab persists. "If I want to, I can walk much faster than you swim. And if I win, you'll never tease anyone again."

Harp laughs at Sea Crab. He doesn't believe that Sea Crab is faster than he is. "Okay, then. If you really are faster, I won't ever tease anyone again."

"Okay," says Sea Crab. "First, we swim past the boulder. Behind it lies a shipwreck. We'll pass that also. Then we turn right and then make another right. There's a seaweed grove that looks exactly like this grove. And there's also the same sign as you see here. That's the finish line."

Harp tries to remember Sea Crab's directions: "Boulder, shipwreck, right, right, finish."

"Ready?" Sea Crab asks, but Harp is already gone.

Harp swims past the boulder and along the side of the shipwreck.
He swerves to the right with a roll, and he turns right again with a double tumbling.
Then he sees the seaweed grove with the plate that Sea Crab talked about.
"Haha! I'm already here!" calls Harp, tapping the plate with his front leg.
But then he sees something strange: Sea Crab is already waiting for him.
"Gosh, Harp, " Sea Crab says. "You're extremely fast, indeed, but not as fast as I am."
Harp was so surprised that he couldn't say a word.
He kept his promise, he never teased anyone again.
Do you want to know how Sea Crab succeeded in beating Harp?
Watch. Those who aren't fast must be smart!

The Harp Seal

Passport

Habitat: in the North Atlantic Ocean

Weight: up to 287 pounds

Height: up to 7 feet

Favorite food: fish, krill, and other crustaceans

About them: male harp seals have a dark brown band over their backs. It looks a bit like the saddle of a horse. That's why they're also called saddleback seals.

Fun fact

Young harp seals have white coats.

The harp seal is a mammal. It can stay underwater for 30 minutes and dive nearly 920 feet deep to catch fish.

A female harp seal can only have one little seal at a time. The young are born on the ice. They don't get cold because of their thick coat.

The milk of a harp seal mom is very thick and very fat. It's a bit like cream.

After two weeks, a small harp seal will no longer receive milk. Its fat becomes muscles. Now it can swim and start catching fish for itself.

Living in a Warm Woolen Mitt

Russian fairy tale,
retold by Marja Baeten

Once upon a time, there was
an old man who was walking
his dog in a large pine forest.
It was extremely cold. His nose turned
red and he began to sneeze. The man grabbed
his handkerchief, and at that moment, he
dropped his woolen mitt. The old man didn't
notice that his mitt had fallen on the ground.
A little field mouse appeared. He saw the mitt
in the snow.

He felt it and thought, *Mmm,
nice and warm.
I want to live in it.*
Not long after, a squirrel arrived.
He asked, "Who lives in this house?"
The field mouse looked outside and said,
"I live here, Mouse Miles. Who are you?"
"I'm Squirrel Ed. May I come in?"
"Of course," said Mouse Miles.
Now they lived together in the woolen mitt.

A moment later, a rabbit passed by. "Who lives in this house?" he asked.

"Mouse Miles and Squirrel Ed. Who are you?"

"Rabbit Hops," said the little rabbit. "Can I live here too?"

The mouse and the squirrel sat closer together, and let the rabbit inside.

Since then, the three of them lived in the woolen mitt.

A sniffing fox came along. "Sniff, sniff," said the fox.

"Does anyone live in this woolen house?"

"Yes, Mouse Miles, Squirrel Ed, and Rabbit Hops. Who are you?"

"I'm Fox Fire Fur. Can I come in?"

The mouse, the squirrel, and the rabbit moved even closer to each other.

From then on, all four of them lived in the woolen mitt.

A bit later, a wolf came by. He asked, "Who lives in this nice and warm house?"

"Mouse Miles, Squirrel Ed, Rabbit Hops, and Fox Fire Fur. Who are you?"

"I'm Wolf Water Tooth. Let me in!"

Quickly the mouse, the squirrel, the rabbit, and the fox moved even closer to each other. From then on, all five of them lived in the woolen mitt. Less than five minutes later, a boar arrived. He asked, "Who lives in this warm woolen house?"

"Mouse Miles, Squirrel Ed, Rabbit Hops, Fox Fire Fur, and Wolf Water Tooth. Who are you?"

"I'm Boar Billy," said the boar. "Are you going to move over so I can get in?"

The animals looked at each other. Would that work? The mouse, the squirrel, the rabbit, the fox, and the wolf thought it was a lovely house. They understood that the boar wanted to be there as well, so they moved even closer to each other. And now all six of them lived in the woolen mitt.

Then a big, brown bear came along.
"Hello, who lives here?" he growled.
"Mouse Miles, Squirrel Ed, Rabbit Hops, Fox Fire Fur, Wolf Water Tooth, and Boar Billy. Who are you?"
"Can't you see? I'm Bear Brown. I can come in, I hope?"
All the animals were even closer to each other. It was now very tight with all seven of them in one woolen mitt! The animals were afraid that the mitt would break . . .

Suddenly the old man came back to look for his woolen mitt. His dog walked forward and barked loudly when he saw it in the distance. The animals in the mitt were so startled by the barking that they jumped out and ran away. And the old man? He was very happy that he could wear his warm mitt again!

The Brown Bear

Passport

Habitat: in the vast forests of northern, cold places
Weight: 220 to 2200 pounds
Height: 7 to 10 feet
Favorite food: honey, fish, plants, and fruits
Abouth them: they often stand on their hind legs to search for food or to impress other animals.

Brown bears have a big nose with which they can smell very well. Sometimes they smell food from more than a mile away.

Brown bears sleep without eating all winter. That's why they eat a lot in the fall. When they wake up, they sometimes weigh only half their normal weight.

Brown bears have strong legs with long claws that they can't retract. With these claws, they can easily remove roots and tubers from the ground. Young bears can climb trees with their claws.

Brown bears like to eat salmon. With a powerful bite or a striking blow with their front leg, they get the fish out of the water.

The Bear, the Goose, and the Winter

Bo Buijs

It's snowing. Thick flakes whirl down.
"Brr!" Bjorn the bear shakes them out of his fur.
He sits next to the river and looks at the sky.
"Sun!" he calls. "Come out and shine!
I want to sunbathe!"
Someone starts laughing behind him.
"The sun isn't coming, silly!"

Bjorn looks around surprised.
Gus the Goose is standing on a hill nearby.
"It'll be winter. In the winter it's freezing,"
she says. "You can prepare for the big draw."
"The big draw?" Bjorn asks. "I can't draw.
I'm a bear."

Gus bursts out laughing again. "You're silly! The big migration! To the south!"

Bjorn shakes his head. He doesn't understand anything about it.

"Come and see," says Gus.

She points over the hill. Curious Bjorn goes to the top of the hill. Then he sees a group of geese. There must be a hundred of them!

"What are they doing?" he asks in amazement.

"They wait until everyone's there," Gus explains. "Our nephews, our nieces, and, of course, our grandfathers and grandmothers. Then we fly to the south. We do that every year. We stay there all winter. It's warm over there, and there's delicious food."

"Oh, really?" Bjorn asks hungrily. "Like what?"

"Grass," says Gus.
Bjorn makes a funny face. "Yuck!"
But Gus is already dreaming away with the idea.
"Pastures full of fresh, juicy, green grass.
We eat it until we have full bellies.
We return here for the spring.
The flight to the south is long,
but . . . it's definitely worth it!"

"What an effort!" Bjorn sighs.
"I spend my winter here, in my warm hole,
under the ground. I sleep a lot . . .
Every now and then my stomach rumbles.
Then I wake up and crawl out of my den
to find food. After that, I sleep nicely.
Until it's spring and the sun is shining again."
He yawns and rubs his eyes, he's suddenly tired.

"Gus!" A goose waddles toward them.
"Everyone's there! We're leaving!"
Gus waves her wing to Bjorn.
"I have to go," she calls. "Bye!"
Bjorn waves back. "Have a safe trip!
Enjoy yourself in the south!"
The group of geese rises. It's a beautiful sight.
Bjorn watches them until they disappear on the horizon.

Then he walks to his den and crawls into it.
Outside it gets colder and colder, but Bjorn
doesn't notice. He sleeps. He dreams of the sun.
Sleep well, Bjorn! Sweet dreams!

35

The Greylag Goose

Passport

Habitat: **near swamps, grasslands, lakes, and other water places**

Weight: **7 to 9 pounds**

Height: **about 3 feet**

Favorite food: **grass, herbs, flowers, and seeds**

About them: **from a distance, the goose's bill looks like a carrot.**

Greylag geese travel to the south in the fall and winter, because there's no fresh grass in Scandinavia and Eastern Europe. They fly back in February, but more and more geese stay in the south year-round.

Greylag geese have sharp teeth along the edges of their bill, so they can easily pick grass.

A female lays four to six eggs once a year. While she sits on her eggs, the male is on guard.

Greylag geese fly in a V-shape during a long distance, so they can save energy.

Where's Puk?

Lucas Arnoldussen

"Come, Puk!" says her mommy, Sil the arctic hare. "I'll take you to Otto the Walrus' house."
"Why?" Puk asks.
"Because I have to go to the forest to find food. You're still too small for that.
Otto will look after you when I'm gone."
"Is Otto the Walrus nice?" Puk asks.
"Very nice," says Mommy Sil.
"Okay, Mommy."

When Mommy Sil and Puk arrive at Otto's home, he's sleeping.
"Woeaahh, good morning," Otto yawns.
"It's already noon!" laughs Puk. "And you're going to take care of me."
"Oh," mumbles Otto. "Well, I'd better get up."
Mommy Sil tells Puk goodbye.
"Stay with Otto, Puk!" she says.
"Yes, Mommy, see you soon!" Puk calls.

When Mommy Sil returns with tree bark and moss, Otto the Walrus is sleeping again. But where's Puk?
"Otto, wake up! Where's Puk?" she asks.
"Well," Otto sighs, "Puk kept talking. I got so tired of it . . . so tired . . . I asked Dora the polar bear if she wanted to look after Puk."
"Let's go there together. Now!" Mommy Sil says angrily.

When they arrive at Dora the Polar Bear's home, Mommy Sil and Otto see two little polar bears playing, but no Puk.
"You're babysitting Puk, right?" Mommy Sil asks Dora. "Yes," she says, "but Puk didn't like it here. My children love to run and play, but Puk just wants to talk. Fortunately, Paco the Arctic Fox wanted to take care of her."
"Then we'll go there together!" sighs Mommy Sil.

Mommy Sil, Otto the Walrus, Dora the Polar Bear, and her two children look for Paco the Arctic Fox.

"Paco! Paaaco! Where are you?" The animals call out.

"Hush," a voice sounds from a mountain of snow. "Here I am. Wait a moment, I'm hunting!"

"Are you looking after Puk?" Mommy Sil whispers.

"Yes, but with all that chatter she drove my prey away."

"Where's Puk now?" Otto the Walrus asks.

"She's playing somewhere over there," Paco replies.

"Then we'll pick her up now!" says Mommy Sil. But Puk isn't playing there or anywhere. Where's Puk?

"We have to look for Puk!" Mommy Sil is worried.

The animals search wherever they can. Otto the Walrus searches in the cold water. Dora the Polar Bear runs with her children across the ice. Paco the Arctic Fox sniffs in and under the snow. Mommy Sil carefully looks under all the trees in the forest.

And they all call: "Puk, where are you?"

Then Mommy Sil hears a heavy voice behind her. "Ahum, Mrs. Arctic Hare? Can I ask you something?" It's the voice of a beautiful reindeer, with huge antlers. "Would you like to take care of this girl? I just found her. She's very sweet, and she loves to talk. We had a great afternoon together, but I'm very busy tonight."

Mommy Sil suddenly sees a little head peeping over the antlers of the reindeer.

"Puk!" Mommy Sil calls out. "Where were you? What were you doing?"

"Talking," Puk says happily. "With Rudolph the Reindeer."

In the evening before bedtime, Puk says, "Mommy, Rudolph says he has to carry a flying sleigh tonight, but I don't believe that!"

"Oh no?" Mommy asks. And she laughs.

She's so happy that her little chatterbox is back.

"Now it's time to be quiet, Puk, and go to sleep."

The Arctic Hare

Fun fact
The paws of an arctic hare are wide, so they don't sink into the snow.

Passport

Habitat: **in the north of Canada and at the North Pole**
Weight: **6 to 15 pounds**
Height: **up to 24 inches**
Favorite food: **tree bark, moss, berries, and leaves**
About them: **the arctic hare can run up to 37 miles per hour.**

The fur of an arctic hare changes color twice a year. In the summer, its coat is gray and brown, and in the winter, its fur is snow-white. Only the tips of its ears always remain black.

A female arctic hare can have about six leverets, or babies. When they're born, their mom quickly sets off again. Once a day she comes by to give them milk.

Arctic hares often travel in large groups, especially in the winter.

The babies leave their mom after a month. The mom soon gets a new litter of babies again.

A Seal of Snow

Geert van Diepen

Too late, thinks Barre the Polar Bear. *The seals are gone.*
He was looking forward to playing hide and seek with them.
The ice has been empty for days. Barre is tired and hungry.
"Hey Barre," he suddenly hears. "Are you okay?"
It's Dirre, the puffin. She flies in the direction of the ice-
cold water.
"I'm alright," says Barre. "How are you?"
"I'm fine!" answers Dirre as she dives underwater with a
plunge. Barre stares gloomily at the circles in the water.
When Dirre comes up again, her bill is full of shiny fish.
One of the fish falls next to Barre in the snow. "Watch it for
me," calls Dirre, "I'll be right back!" And she's gone again.

Barre looks at the delicious fish. He's starving.
His belly rumbles; his mouth is watering.
He hasn't eaten in days.
Oh, that fish looks so tasty. Dirre wouldn't mind
if he ate it, would she?
Of course not, Barre decides.
Suddenly he hears Dirre. "Here I am again!
Thanks for taking care of the fish!"
Barre looks sad.
"Is something wrong?" asks Dirre. "You can tell
me."

"I think about seals a lot lately," says Barre. "But
I don't see them anymore. I search and search. I
swim and swim . . ."
"Stop searching," says Dirre. "I have a better idea.
Why don't you make a seal yourself . . . of snow!"
"A seal?" asks Barre. "Of snow?"
Dirre takes the fallen fish in her bill. "Yes," she
calls as she flies away. "You know what they look
like!"

Barre thinks for one hour. Then he starts working. He collects snow and makes the head of a seal. He makes the eyes using two black stones and the whiskers using two small branches. Then he makes the body of the seal and attaches the head to it. He finally adds flippers on the sides.

"Oh, Barre!" says Dirre when she comes to have a look.

"You did such a great job. It looks very real!"

Yes, agrees Barre, his seal is well made. His mouth is watering again.

"What's next?"

"Now you must sit there behind the ice," says Dirre. "Very quietly."

Barre does what Dirre says. He watches from a distance.

Dirre walks to the seal made of snow and hides herself behind its back.

"Wooo!" she says. "Wooo, wooo!"

Gee! Barre is surprised. He knows that sound. It's how seals call each other.

And now Dirre imitates that sound. How clever of her!

"Wooo, wooo!"

Will the seals in the water hear it? Barre looks at the water, but he doesn't see any movement.

Or does he? Suddenly a little round head appears in the water. And another one

and another one. The seals are curiously looking at the white seal on the ice.

"You did it, Dirre," whispers Barre. "I see more than ten seals!" They all climb onto the ice.

How nice, thinks Barre the Polar Bear. Now he can finally play hide and seek with them again!

The Polar Bear

Passport

Habitat: on the ice of the North Pole

Weight: a male weighs up to 2200 pounds, a female up to 660 pounds

Height: up to 10 feet when standing or 5 feet on all fours

Favorite food: seals, especially their fat

About them: they can smell a dead animal from 20 miles away.

Fun fact

The polar bear is the only bear that always eats meat.

A female polar bear usually gives birth to twins. The cubs are bald and blind when they're born and not much heavier than a rat. They stay with their mother for three years.

Polar bears often wait to catch a seal at a hole in the ice. Seals must come up for air occasionally and when they do, polar bears are waiting to catch them for dinner.

A polar bear is never cold. A layer of fat provides extra warmth under the skin. That's especially nice when the polar bear is swimming in ice-cold water.

A polar bear has a white coat, but the skin under that coat is completely black!

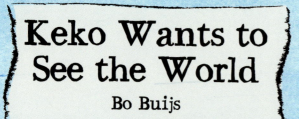

Keko Wants to See the World

Bo Buijs

Morgan is a small killer whale. His big sister Keko wants to show
him something. She tells him to follow her as they swim together.
"Don't go too far," says Mommy.
"Don't worry. We'll be back in a minute!" replies Keko.
They swim to the edge of the bay. There's the sea.
There are waves as far as they can see. Far away is a small island.
Behind that island is more sea.
"Look!" says Keko. "Here starts the rest of the world.
When I grow up, I want to see the world. I can't wait!"
"But if you want to see the world, you can't see Mommy
for a long time," says Morgan.
"Oh, that's okay," laughs Keko.
"I can go awhile without her."

In the distance is an ice floe on the waves. There's someone standing on it.
"It looks like a reindeer," says Morgan. "A small one!"
Keko dives into the waves and swims towards it. "Come on!" She calls to Morgan.
"Aren't we going too far away from Mommy?" Morgan says.
"Don't worry. We'll be right back!" Keko shouts.
"All right," says Morgan. He swims with her.
"Hey there!" Keko says to the reindeer. "What are you doing here?"
"I wanted to watch the fish," the reindeer explains.
"I was close to the water, but then the ice broke off where I stood!"
And then his paws begin to sink through the ice. "I want to go home!"

51

"We'll help you," says Keko. "Where do you live?"

The reindeer nods toward the island in the distance.

Morgan says that it's far, but Keko is bold.

"Okay," she says. "We've already discovered some of the world."

She puts her nose to the ice floe and starts pushing it.

"Aren't we going too far away from Mommy?" asks Morgan.

"Don't worry," says Keko again. "We'll be right back."

She pushes and pushes, but it isn't easy. The waves are high, and the wind blows the ice floe in the wrong direction.

"Okay," sighs Morgan as he helps his sister.

Finally, the ice floe moves the right way.

BANK! The ice floe finally bumps onto the shore.
The little reindeer jumps off and runs to his mommy and daddy.
They're so happy to be together again! They give each other a big hug.
"They hug him just like Mommy hugs us," says Morgan.
"Yes, just like Mommy . . ." nods Keko.
 She suddenly misses her mother so badly that she starts to cry.
"Don't be sad," says Morgan. "We'll be home soon."

They swim back to the bay as fast as they can.
Keko doesn't think about the rest of the world now.
She'll discover it later. And later will last for a very long time . . .

The Killer Whale

Passport

Habitat: in seas worldwide

Weight: from 5730 to 19,840 pounds

Length (with tail): males 26 to 33 feet, females 23 to 28 feet

Favorite food: all large sea animals, including whales

About them: females can live to be 80 years old, and males can live to be 60 years old.

The killer whale is a very large dolphin. It can be recognized by its striking black-and-white drawing on his high dorsal fin.

Killer whales usually live in a group and the oldest female is in charge. She's the mother of most killer whales in the group.

Each group makes its own sounds. The killer whales recognize each other. They also go hunting as a group.

To catch a seal, a killer whale sometimes swims near the ice or the beach.

Rodi's Great Antlers
Lucas Arnoldussen

"Those antlers of yours aren't growing very quickly, are they?" Rodi's daddy teases him playfully. "Look, even your sister has them already." Rodi looks down sadly. Daddy is right. Her antlers look like two little bumps now, but they're definitely growing. "Don't worry," says Daddy. "Your antlers will come too." Rodi hears laughter behind him. He turns around. It's Dorian and his friends. They also have antlers.

They laugh at Rodi because he has none. "Wait and see," Rodi cries. "I will have such big antlers that you'll be scared of them!" "And when will that be?" Dorian laughs. "Well . . ." Rodi hesitates. "Well . . . tomorrow!" Dorian and his friends scream with laughter. "We have to see it!" they shout. "Tomorrow at sunrise in the clearing!"

A bit later, Rodi is
walking through
the forest.
He regrets what he said.
No one gets antlers in one
night, and he knows that.
Rodi is mad at Dorian, mad
at his antlers that won't grow,
and mad at himself. He's so mad
that he kicks a tree with his hind legs.
Something falls on Rodi's head. "Ouch!" he calls.
There's a squirrel on the ground before him.
"Couldn't you kick against another tree?"
"Sorry," Rodi murmurs. "I was mad because I don't have any antlers."
"How's that possible?" asks the squirrel. "Let me see."
The squirrel climbs on top of Rodi's head. "There's really a bump
here, you know," says the squirrel happily.
"Yes, but that's not an antler," grumbles Rodi. "I have that bump
on my head because you fell on it." Rodi tells the squirrel about
his antlers, about Dorian and his friends, and about their meeting
in the clearing tomorrow.

"Maybe I can help you," the squirrel says.

"Well, only if you know how I can get antlers in one night," says Rodi.

"Unfortunately, I can't practice magic," says the squirrel.

"But I have a good idea! We're going to scare that Dorian.

Wait, I'll be right back!" Quickly the squirrel climbs up the tall tree.

Rodi is waiting until he hears a voice from above: "Watch out!"

Rodi just avoids the two big branches falling from the tree.

"Hey, be careful! I already have a big bump on my head," he calls.

"Sorry!" the squirrel laughs. "But this is part of the plan. Watch!"

The next morning, Dorian and his friends are already in the clearing. They chuckle and laugh at Rodi. "An antler in one night? What does he think he is?" they laugh.

When the first rays of sunlight rise above the trees, the reindeer friends suddenly hear a voice behind them. It's Rodi's voice.

"Take a good look, Dorian. Today I have the biggest antlers of us all! You didn't expect that, did you?"

And indeed. The reindeer look surprised.
On top of the hill, in the sunlight, is Rodi . . .
with huge antlers! How's that possible?
How did he do it? What happened?
The reindeer run in all directions.

On the top of the hill, the squirrel screeches happily.
"They believed it!" Rodi cries.
"These branches look like real antlers!"
"But you don't need those branches anymore,"
says the squirrel. "Because now I don't see just one,
but two bumps. And I don't think something has fallen
on your head twice, right?"

59

The Reindeer

Passport

Habitat: **in America, Europe, and Asia, close to the North Pole**

Weight: **265 to 660 pounds**

Length: **4 to 7 feet**

Shoulder height: **up to 5 feet**

Favorite food: **grass, herbs, moss, lichen, and mushrooms**

About them: **the antlers always have a forward-facing branch.**

Fun fact
A reindeer from North America is called a caribou.

The reindeer is the only deer whose females also have antlers. However, the antlers of the males are a lot bigger.

The hooves of a reindeer have widely spread toes. With this, they sink less quickly into swampy soil and into the snow.

Reindeer make a long trek twice a year in search of food. They do this in large herds of up to 100,000 reindeer.

The trek can be more than 1200 miles long!